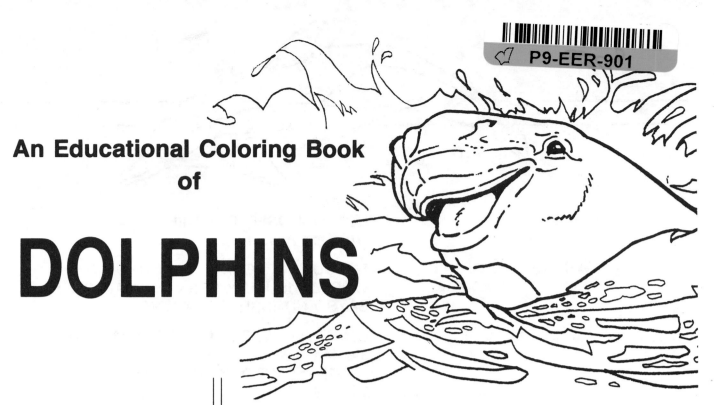

An Educational Coloring Book
of
DOLPHINS

EDITOR
Linda Spizzirri

ILLUSTRATIONS
Peter M. Spizzirri

COVER ART
Peter M. Spizzirri

CONTENTS

An Educational Coloring Book of DOLPHINS • Published by SPIZZIRRI PUBLISHING, INC., P.O. BOX 9397, RAPID CITY, SOUTH DAKOTA 57709. No part of this publication may be reproduced by any means without the express written consent of the publisher. All national and international rights reserved on the entire contents of this publication.
Printed in U.S.A.

NAME:	BOTTLE-NOSED DOLPHIN *(Tursiops truncatus)*
WHERE IT LIVES:	FOUND IN OCEANS AROUND THE WORLD. USUALLY SEEN IN SHALLOW BAYS AND INSHORE WATERS
SIZE:	LENGTH: 5½ TO 12 FEET (1¾ TO 3½ M.) WEIGHT: 331 TO 441 POUNDS (150 TO 200 KG.)
WHAT IT EATS:	A VARIETY OF FISH, SHARKS, SHRIMP, RAYS, AND SQUID.
COLOR IT:	BLACK, BLUE-BLACK, OR GRAY ABOVE; LIGHTER BELOW
INTERESTING FACTS:	The "Bottle-nosed" dolphin got its name because its sharp beak looks like the top of an old fashioned bottle. They are very fast swimmers capable of speeds up to 20 knots (23 m.p.h.). It is the most common dolphin off the east coast of the United States. This dolphin is easily trained in captivity and performs in water shows at zoos, aquariums, marine lands and sea-life parks. A female is usually six years old before she can bear young. The young do not quickly transfer from milk to fish feeding. It is known that they can remain milk fed for as long as eighteen months.

NAME:	SPINNER DOLPHIN *(Stenella longirostris)*
WHERE IT LIVES:	TROPICAL WATERS WORLD WIDE
SIZE:	APPROXIMATELY 6½ FEET (2 M.)
WHAT IT EATS:	MOSTLY FISH
COLOR IT:	BLUE-BLACK UPPER BODY, LIGHT COLORED BELLY
INTERESTING FACTS:	This dolphin was so named because of its beautiful aerial spin. In a split second the magnificently agile creature can jump from the water and spin two and one half times around the axis of its body. It is not clear why the dolphin does this spin. Besides eating surface fish, it is known that the Spinner dolphin feeds on deep sea smelt that is more than 800 feet below the surface.

NAME:	KILLER WHALE *(Orcinus orca)*
WHERE IT LIVES:	MOST COMMON IN THE ARCTIC AND ANTARCTIC, BUT FOUND IN ALL OTHER OCEANS
SIZE:	LENGTH: 19½ FEET (6 M.) WEIGHT: 2205 POUNDS (1000 KG.)
WHAT IT EATS:	BIRDS, SEALS, BALEEN WHALES, SEA OTTER, FISH, SQUID, AND OCTOPUS
COLOR IT:	BLACK WITH WHITE PATCHES, WHITE BELLY
INTERESTING FACTS:	The Killer whale isn't a whale at all, and it isn't a killer, either, as far as man is concerned. It is the biggest of the dolphins, with a large dorsal (top) fin that sticks out of the water like a pole. Besides this large dorsal fin, the Killer whale can be identified by his rounded snout and the white patch above its eye. The dolphins swim in packs of up to 50 members. They are probably the fastest swimmers of all dolphins, with speeds that reach 26 knots (30 m.p.h.), and they can jump high into the air. If prey is spotted in icey areas, they can break through ice that is as much as 1 meter (3 feet) thick, to knock the bird or animal into the water.

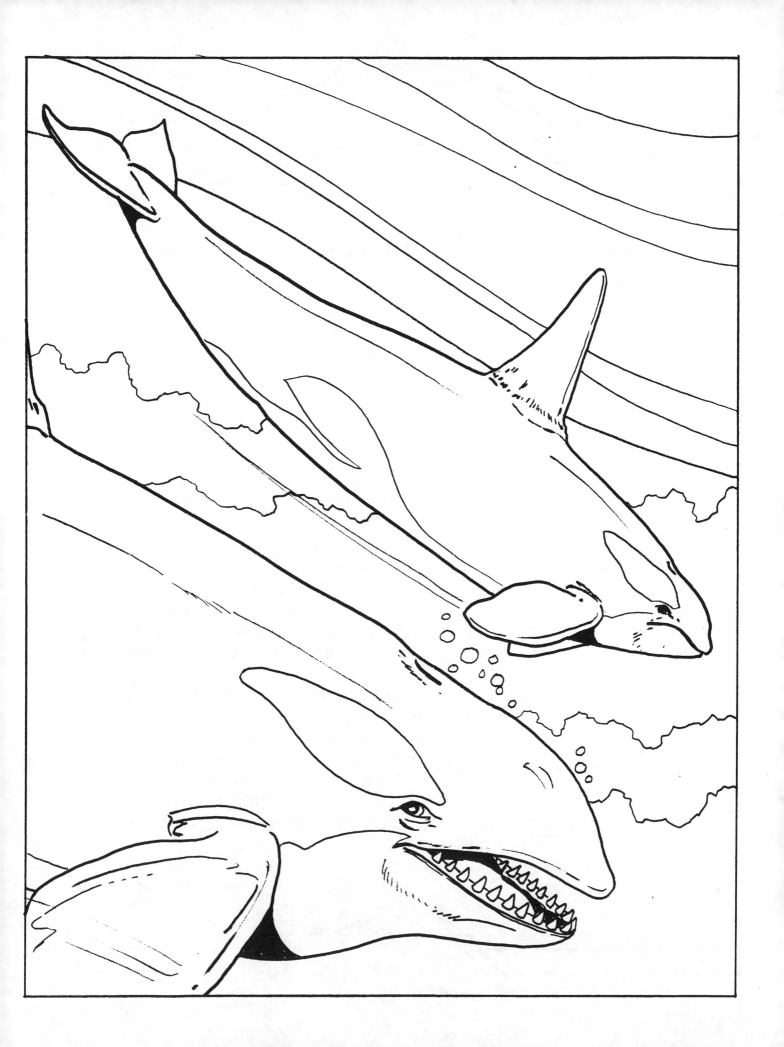

NAME:	RISSO'S DOLPHIN *(Grampus griseus)*
WHERE IT LIVES:	WEST AND EAST COAST OF THE UNITED STATES, THE NORTH ATLANTIC, MEDITERRANEAN SEA, RED SEA, THE COASTS OF JAPAN, CHINA, AUSTRALIA, NEW ZEALAND, AND SOUTH AFRICA
SIZE:	LENGTH: 13 FEET (4 M.)
WHAT IT EATS:	FISH, SQUID, OCTOPUSES, AND CUTTLEFISH
COLOR IT:	GRAYISH-BLUE OR BLACK ABOVE, LIGHTER BELOW, FINS AND TAIL ARE BLACK
INTERESTING FACTS:	Risso's dolphins swim in small groups, usually less than a dozen. Sometimes several of the small groups join. They jump and play, sometimes doing belly flops into the water. These dolphins don't have very many teeth, and have no beak at all.

Pelorus Jack was the nickname given to one famous Risso's dolphin, who was even protected by the New Zealand government. He would guide ships into the area known as Pelorus Sound. Because he was seen from 1896 to 1916, we know that dolphins can get quite old.

NAME:	ROUGH TOOTHED DOLPHIN *(Steno Bredanensis)*
WHERE IT LIVES:	WARM WATERS OF THE ATLANTIC, PACIFIC, AND INDIAN OCEANS, RED, MEDITERRANEAN, AND CARIBBEAN SEAS
SIZE:	LENGTH: 5½ TO 8 FEET (1¾ TO 2½ M.)
WHAT IT EATS:	FISH, CUTTLEFISH, SQUID
COLOR IT:	BLUE-BLACK OR PURPLE-BLACK UPPER WITH SCATTERED MARKINGS, PINK OR ROSE BELLY, BLUE-BLACK SPOTS, WHITE BEAK
INTERESTING FACTS:	This little known dolphin has been seen only in warm water. It gets it's name from the rough surface of its teeth. The teeth numbering 40 to 54 on each side of its jaw, have rough ridges plus deep wrinkles and grooves. Not very much is known about how they live and behave. Like their relatives, the whales, dolphins breathe through a blowhole. The blowhole is located at the top of their head.

NAME:	PACIFIC STRIPED DOLPHIN (*Lagenorhynchus obliquidens*)
WHERE IT LIVES:	OCEANS AROUND THE WORLD
SIZE:	LENGTH: 5 TO 10 FEET (1½ TO 3 M.) WEIGHT: 165 POUNDS (75 KG.)
WHAT IT EATS:	FISH, CRUSTACEANS, (SHRIMP, CRAB, LOBSTER), SQUIDS AND WHELKS
COLOR IT:	BLACK OR GRAY ABOVE, LIGHTER BELOW, GRAY STREAKS ON SIDES.
INTERESTING FACTS:	It is easy to tell a Pacific striped dolphin because it has a very short beak, a pointed dorsal fin and pointed flippers. Sometimes the dolphins will travel for long distances looking for food, and have been known to travel with pilot whales. The related species of Pacific striped dolphins live in the open seas in small schools. Sometimes the animals will join into a larger school that divides when the animals feed.

NAME:	COMMERSON'S DOLPHIN *(Cephalorhynchus commersonnii)*
WHERE IT LIVES:	SOUTHERN OCEANS
SIZE:	LENGTH: 4 TO 6 FEET (1 TO 2 M.)
WHAT IT EATS:	CUTTLEFISH AND SHRIMP
COLOR IT:	CONTRASTING PATTERNS OF BLACK AND WHITE
INTERESTING FACTS:	This colorful family of dolphins lives in colder waters of the southern oceans. Their contrasting black and white patterns make them easily noticed from the decks of ships. They are seen swimming in large schools. They do not have the beak like many other dolphins. There are four kinds of dolphins in this family. Although they are seen often, not very much is known about them.

NAME:	COMMON DOLPHIN *(Delphinus delphis)*
WHERE IT LIVES:	WORLD-WIDE OCEANS, WARM SEAS, AND SOMETIMES IN COLD OR FRESH WATER.
SIZE:	LENGTH: 5 TO 8 FEET (1½ TO 2½ M.) WEIGHT: 165 POUNDS (75 KG.)
WHAT IT EATS:	FISH, FLYING FISH, SQUID, AND OCTOPUS
COLOR IT:	BROWN OR BLACK BACK, WHITE BELLY, BANDS OF WHITE, GRAY, OR YELLOW ON THE SIDES.
INTERESTING FACTS:	The Common dolphin is easily identified by its distinctive narrow beak which is set off sharply from the forehead by a deep V-shaped groove. The jaw of each of these dolphins contains from 80 to 100 teeth. These lively swimmers usually travel at 5 knots, (6 m.p.h.) but, because they are capable of speeds up to 25 knots, (29 m.p.h.), they have the distinction of being one of the fastest moving dolphins.

NAME:	RIGHT WHALE DOLPHIN *(Lissodelphis borealis)*
WHERE IT LIVES:	FROM JAPAN TO CALIFORNIA IN THE NORTHERN PACIFIC OCEAN
SIZE:	LENGTH: 8 FEET (2½ M.)
WHAT IT EATS:	FISH, CUTTLEFISH, OCTOPUS, AND SQUID
COLOR IT:	BLACK UPPER PARTS, FLIPPERS AND TAIL; WHITE UNDER PARTS
INTERESTING FACTS:	The Right whale dolphin was so named, because like the bowhead whale, it doesn't have a dorsal (back) fin, as do most of the dolphins and whales. There are two species of Right whale dolphins. This one lives in the northern Pacific and the other lives in the southern seas. The northern species is about a foot longer than its southern cousin. These dolphins live far out to sea, and swim in small groups or schools. They swim very fast and change direction quickly. They often jump out of the water. They have short beaks and small sharp teeth.

NAME:	AMAZON DOLPHIN (*Inia geoffrensis*)
WHERE IT LIVES:	AMAZON AND ORINOCO RIVERS IN SOUTH AMERICA
SIZE:	LENGTH: 6½ TO 10 FEET (2 TO 3 M.) WEIGHT: 276 POUNDS (125 KG.)
WHAT IT EATS:	FISH
COLOR IT:	YOUNG: GRAYISH OR BLACK UPPER PARTS, LIGHTER GRAY UNDER PARTS. OLD: PALE PINK OR FLESH COLORED
INTERESTING FACTS:	The Amazon dolphin has a long, slender beak that probes the muddy river bottom for fish to eat. It rolls over to breathe, when it is feeding or swimming rapidly. Some of the animals use a kind of sonar to find big objects in the muddy water. Sometimes the Amazon dolphin leaps high out of the water. Even though it appears to look around when it jumps out of the water, it's vision isn't very good.

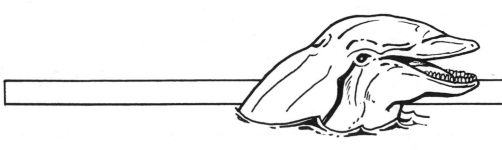

NAME:	IRRAWADDY RIVER DOLPHIN *(Orcaella brevirostris)*
WHERE IT LIVES:	THE IRRAWADDY RIVER OF BURMA AND THE WARM COASTAL WATERS OF SOUTHEASTERN ASIA
SIZE:	LENGTH: 6½ TO 8 FEET (2 TO 2½ M.)
WHAT IT EATS:	FISH
COLOR IT:	BLUE-BLACK OR BLUE-GRAY THROUGHOUT. THE BELLY MAY BE SLIGHTLY LIGHTER.
INTERESTING FACTS:	The Irrawaddy River dolphin has a bulging forehead, and a mouth shape that gives the impresssion that it is smiling. Fishermen in Burma like this dolphin, and believe that it leads schools of fish into their nets. Schools of dolphins swim beside ships and are thought to be good luck. They come to the surface to breathe, every one or two minutes. Their heads can be seen at the beginning of a breath, then their backs. Their tails stay in the water most of the time. They rarely leap out of the water like many of the dolphins do. Some people believe that oil from the dolphin can cure rheumatism.

NAME:	WHITE DOLPHIN (*Sousa teuszii*)
WHERE IT LIVES:	CAMEROONS AND SENEGAL, WEST AFRICA
SIZE:	LENGTH: 4 TO 8 FEET (1 to 2½ M.) WEIGHT: 287 POUNDS (130 KG.)
WHAT IT EATS:	ONLY FISH
COLOR IT:	BROWN, GRAY OR BLACK ABOVE; LIGHTER BELLY
INTERESTING FACTS:	The White dolphin only lives in warm waters, but doesn't seem to mind if it is fresh or salt water. There are five species of white dolphins. They live around China, India, and parts of Africa. They have a long nose called a beak, plus, from 92 to 148 teeth. The White dolphin is identified by its long beak, broad flippers, and triangular dorsal (top) fin. They swim more slowly than most dolphins. They roll in the water when breathing, and appear to roll more rapidly when they are feeding.

NAME:	RIVER DOLPHINS *(Sotalia brasiliensis)*
WHERE IT LIVES:	THE BAY OF RIO DE JANEIRO
SIZE:	LENGTH: 3 TO 5 FEET (1 TO 1½ M.) WEIGHT: 106 POUNDS (48 KG.)
WHAT IT EATS:	FISH AND SOME SHRIMP
COLOR IT:	PALE BLUE-GRAY TO BLACK ABOVE, YELLOWISH-ORANGE SIDES, WHITE BELOW. BRIGHT YELLOW SPOT NEAR TOP OF DORSAL FIN.
INTERESTING FACTS:	This South American dolphin is considered sacred by the natives. They believe the River dolphins to be mans friend, and even to be responsible for drowned bodies being brought to shore. They faithfully protect their "friends."

Even though this species is only found in the Rio de Janeiro bay area, other river dolphins are found in fresh water rivers and lakes. The river dolphin has a very streamline appearance because its forehead is not very pronounced and it has a slender beak. These graceful animals move rather slowly. Every movement is so perfect, they can swim in tight formation, breathe, and roll so close to each other that they can almost touch. They do not usually band together in groups of more than eight.

NAME:	GANGES DOLPHIN *(Platanista gangetica)*
WHERE IT LIVES:	THE RIVERS OF NORTHERN INDIA
SIZE:	LENGTH: 6½ TO 10 FEET (2 TO 3 M.)
WHAT IT EATS:	FISH, SHRIMP, AND FRESHWATER ORGANISMS
COLOR IT:	DARK GRAY OR BLACK BACK, THE BELLY IS LIGHTER
INTERESTING FACTS:	The Ganges dolphin lives in the Ganges River in India, moving upriver as far as it can go. It apparently never moves into salt water oceans, but spends its entire life in fresh water. It has a long beak in front of a sharp forehead. The Ganges dolphin is distinguished by its small dorsal (top) fin, its short blunt flippers, and two plates of bone that stick out and nearly touch in front of the blowhole. The animal breathes every two and a half minutes by plunging out of the water while leaping forward. It is blind, and uses its sensitive beak to find fish and shrimp in the muddy river bottom. The animal is curious, and seems to be unafraid around people. Usually, three to ten Ganges dolphins form a school, and swim up and down the rivers together.

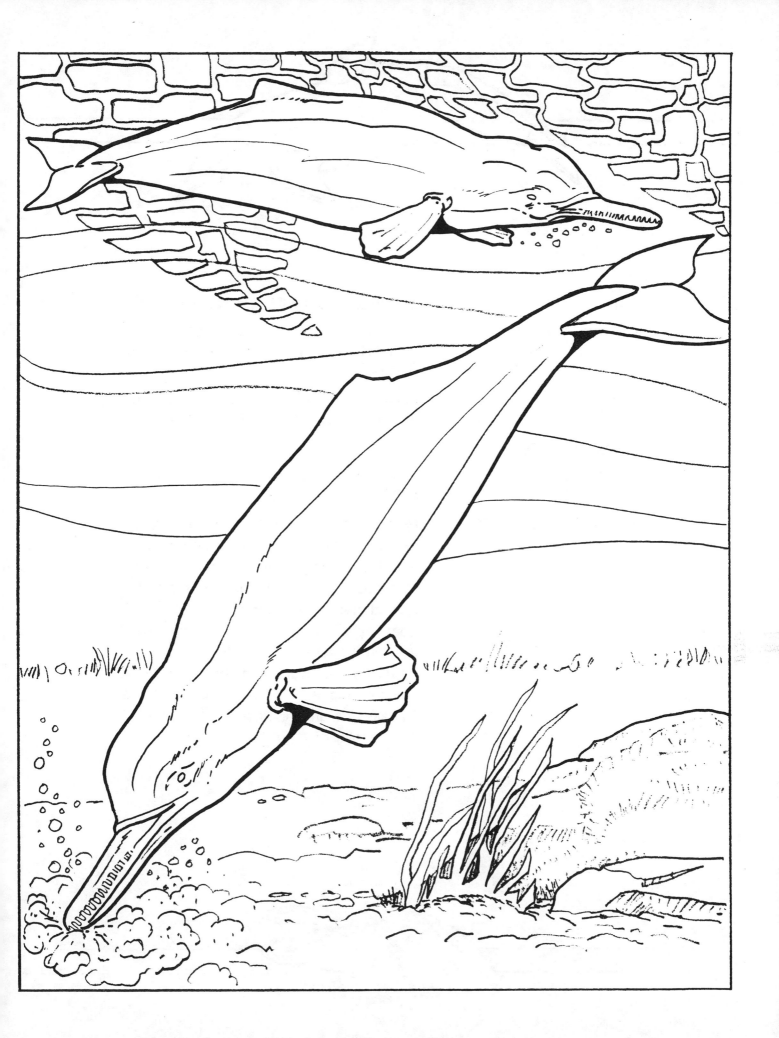

NAME:	CHINESE DOLPHIN *(Lipotes vexillifer)*
WHERE IT LIVES:	TUNGTING LAKE, AND NEAR THE MOUTH OF THE YANGTZE RIVER IN CHINA
SIZE:	LENGTH: 6½ TO 8 FEET (2 TO 2½ M.) WEIGHT: 353 POUNDS (160 KG.)
WHAT IT EATS:	FISH
COLOR IT:	PALE BLUE-GRAY ABOVE, WHITE BELOW
INTERESTING FACTS:	Because the Chinese dolphin's long beak-like snout curves upward, it almost looks like it is smiling. The long snout is used to probe the river bottom for food. The animal has a very small eye, and very poor eyesight. After spring rains have swollen the lakes, the Chinese dolphin will travel up the rivers from the lake where it lives, and may have its babies there. Usually, the animals travel in little groups, or schools, of 3 to 12 animals.

AWARD WINNERS
SPIZZIRRI PUBLISHING, INC.

100 Best Childrens Products Award COLOR BOOK/CASSETTES

Factual information, dramatic narration, sound effects and music make these cassettes and books a special learning experience every child will remember with pleasure.

THREE CASSETTE LIBRARY ALBUM
YOUR CHOICE OF 3 STORY CASSETTES AND BOOKS IN A PLASTIC STORAGE CASE
SPI 222-9

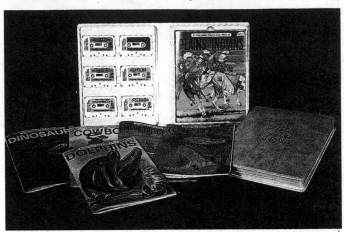

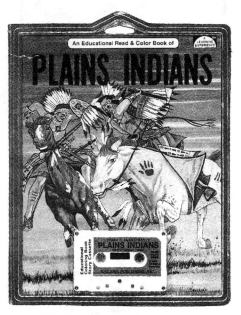

INDIVIDUAL BOOK AND CASSETTE PACKAGE

SIX CASSETTE LIBRARY ALBUM
YOUR CHOICE OF 6 STORY CASSETTES AND BOOKS IN A PLASTIC STORAGE CASE
SPI 169-9

INDIVIDUALLY BOXED CASSETTES
All cassettes are in reusable plastic cases.
SPI 224-5

48 DIFFERENT TITLES TO CHOOSE FROM
ALL INDIVIDUAL CASSETTE AND BOOK PACKAGES

SPI 109-5 AIRCRAFT	SPI 152-4 COWBOYS	SPI 091-9 NORTHWEST INDIANS	SPI 101-X REPTILES
SPI 096-X ANIMAL ALPHABET	SPI 107-9 DEEP-SEA FISH	SPI 149-4 PACIFIC FISH	SPI 114-1 ROCKETS
SPI 104-4 ANIMAL GIANTS	SPI 082-X DINOSAURS	SPI 147-8 PENGUINS	SPI 105-2 SHARKS
SPI 148-6 ATLANTIC FISH	SPI 161-3 DOGS	SPI 151-6 PIONEERS	SPI 156-7 SHIPS
SPI 159-1 BIRDS	SPI 095-1 DOLLS	SPI 089-7 PLAINS INDIANS	SPI 092-7 SOUTHEAST INDIANS
SPI 094-3 CALIFORNIA INDIANS	SPI 108-7 DOLPHINS	SPI 112-5 PLANETS	SPI 093-5 SOUTHWEST INDIANS
SPI 160-5 CATS	SPI 103-6 ENDANG'D SPECIES	SPI 158-3 POISONOUS SNAKES	SPI 110-9 SPACE CRAFT
SPI 102-8 CATS OF THE WILD	SPI 153-2 ESKIMOS	SPI 084-6 PREHIST. BIRD	SPI 111-7 SPACE EXPLORERS
SPI 085-4 CAVEMAN	SPI 154-0 FARM ANIMALS	SPI 086-2 PREHIST. FISH	SPI 098-6 STATE BIRDS
SPI 150-8 COLONIES	SPI 162-1 HORSES	SPI 087-0 PREH. MAMMALS	SPI 163-X STATE FLOWERS
SPI 113-3 COMETS	SPI 100-1 MAMMALS	SPI 083-8 PREHIST. SEA LIFE	SPI 155-9 TRANSPORTATION
SPI 097-8 Count/Color DINOSAURS	SPI 090-0 NORTHEAST INDIANS	SPI 157-5 PRIMATES	SPI 106-0 WHALES

SPI 480-9   48 CASSETTE AND BOOK ASSORTMENT